THE JPS B'NAI MITZVAH TORAH COMMENTARY

Balak (Numbers 22:2–25:9)
Haftarah (Micah 5:6–6:8)

Rabbi Jeffrey K. Salkin

The Jewish Publication Society · Philadelphia
University of Nebraska Press · Lincoln

INTRODUCTION

News flash: the most important thing about becoming bar or bat mitzvah isn't the party. Nor is it the presents. Nor even being able to celebrate with your family and friends—as wonderful as those things are. Nor is it even standing before the congregation and reading the prayers of the liturgy—as important as that is.

No, the most important thing about becoming bar or bat mitzvah is sharing Torah with the congregation. And why is that? Because of all Jewish skills, that is the most important one.

Here is what is true about rites of passage: you can tell what a culture values by the tasks it asks its young people to perform on their way to maturity. In American culture, you become responsible for driving, responsible for voting, and yes, responsible for drinking responsibly.

In some cultures, the rite of passage toward maturity includes some kind of trial, or a test of strength. Sometimes, it is a kind of "outward bound" camping adventure. Among the Maasai tribe in Africa, it is traditional for a young person to hunt and kill a lion. In some Hispanic cultures, fifteen year-old girls celebrate the *quinceañera*, which marks their entrance into maturity.

What is Judaism's way of marking maturity? It combines both of these rites of passage: *responsibility* and *test*. You show that you are on your way to becoming a *responsible* Jewish adult through a public *test* of strength and knowledge—reading or chanting Torah, and then teaching it to the congregation.

This is the most important Jewish ritual mitzvah (commandment), and that is how you demonstrate that you are, truly, bar or bat mitzvah—old enough to be responsible for the mitzvot.

What Is Torah?

So, what exactly is the Torah? You probably know this already, but let's review.

The Torah (teaching) consists of "the five books of Moses," sometimes also called the *chumash* (from the Hebrew word *chameish*, which means "five"), or, sometimes, the Greek word Pentateuch (which means "the five teachings").

Here are the five books of the Torah, with their common names and their Hebrew names.

› **Genesis (The beginning), which in Hebrew is Bere'shit (from the first words—"When God began to create").** Bere'shit spans the years from Creation to Joseph's death in Egypt. Many of the Bible's best stories are in Genesis: the creation story itself; Adam and Eve in the Garden of Eden; Cain and Abel; Noah and the Flood; and the tales of the Patriarchs and Matriarchs, Abraham, Isaac, Jacob, Sarah, Rebekah, Rachel, and Leah. It also includes one of the greatest pieces of world literature, the story of Joseph, which is actually the oldest complete novel in history, comprising more than one-quarter of all Genesis.

› **Exodus (Getting out), which in Hebrew is Shemot (These are the names).** Exodus begins with the story of the Israelite slavery in Egypt. It then moves to the rise of Moses as a leader, and the Israelites' liberation from slavery. After the Israelites leave Egypt, they experience the miracle of the parting of the Sea of Reeds (or "Red Sea"); the giving of the Ten Commandments at Mount Sinai; the idolatry of the Golden Calf; and the design and construction of the Tabernacle and of the ark for the original tablets of the law, which our ancestors carried with them in the desert. Exodus also includes various ethical and civil laws, such as "You shall not wrong a stranger or oppress him, for you were strangers in the land of Egypt" (22:20).

› **Leviticus (about the Levites), or, in Hebrew, Va-yikra' (And God called).** It goes into great detail about the kinds of sacrifices that the ancient Israelites brought as offerings; the laws of ritual purity; the animals that were permitted and forbidden for eating (the beginnings of the tradition of kashrut, the Jewish dietary laws); the diagnosis of various skin diseases; the ethical laws of holiness; the ritual calendar of the Jewish year; and various agricultural laws concerning the treatment of the Land of Israel. Leviticus is basically the manual of ancient Judaism.

> Numbers (because the book begins with the census of the Israelites), or, in Hebrew, Be-midbar (In the wilderness). The book describes the forty years of wandering in the wilderness and the various rebellions against Moses. The constant theme: "Egypt wasn't so bad. Maybe we should go back." The greatest rebellion against Moses was the negative reports of the spies about the Land of Israel, which discouraged the Israelites from wanting to move forward into the land. For that reason, the "wilderness generation" must die off before a new generation can come into maturity and finish the journey.

> Deuteronomy (The repetition of the laws of the Torah), or, in Hebrew, Devarim (The words). The final book of the Torah is, essentially, Moses's farewell address to the Israelites as they prepare to enter the Land of Israel. Here we find various laws that had been previously taught, though sometimes with different wording. Much of Deuteronomy contains laws that will be important to the Israelites as they enter the Land of Israel—laws concerning the establishment of a monarchy and the ethics of warfare. Perhaps the most famous passage from Deuteronomy contains the *Shema*, the declaration of God's unity and uniqueness, and the *Ve-ahavta,* which follows it. Deuteronomy ends with the death of Moses on Mount Nebo as he looks across the Jordan Valley into the land that he will not enter.

Jews read the Torah in sequence—starting with Bere'shit right after Simchat Torah in the autumn, and then finishing Devarim on the following Simchat Torah. Each Torah portion is called a parashah (division; sometimes called a *sidrah,* a place in the order of the Torah reading). The stories go around in a full circle, reminding us that we can always gain more insights and more wisdom from the Torah. This means that if you don't "get" the meaning this year, don't worry—it will come around again.

And What Else? The Haftarah

We read or chant the Torah from the Torah scroll—the most sacred thing that a Jewish community has in its possession. The Torah is written without vowels, and the ability to read it and chant it is part of the challenge and the test.

But there is more to the synagogue reading. Every Torah reading has an accompanying haftarah reading. Haftarah means "conclusion," because there was once a time when the service actually ended with that reading. Some scholars believe that the reading of the haftarah originated at a time when non-Jewish authorities outlawed the reading of the Torah, and the Jews read the haftarah sections instead. In fact, in some synagogues, young people who become bar or bat mitzvah read very little Torah and instead read the entire haftarah portion.

The haftarah portion comes from the Nevi'im, the prophetic books, which are the second part of the Jewish Bible. It is either read or chanted from a Hebrew Bible, or maybe from a booklet or a photocopy.

The ancient sages chose the haftarah passages because their themes reminded them of the words or stories in the Torah text. Sometimes, they chose *haftarah* with special themes in honor of a festival or an upcoming festival.

Not all books in the prophetic section of the Hebrew Bible consist of prophecy. Several are historical. For example:

The book of Joshua tells the story of the conquest and settlement of Israel.

The book of Judges speaks of the period of early tribal rulers who would rise to power, usually for the purpose of uniting the tribes in war against their enemies. Some of these leaders are famous: Deborah, the great prophetess and military leader, and Samson, the biblical strong man.

The books of Samuel start with Samuel, the last judge, and then move to the creation of the Israelite monarchy under Saul and David (approximately 1000 BCE).

The books of Kings tell of the death of King David, the rise of King Solomon, and how the Israelite kingdom split into the Northern Kingdom of Israel and the Southern Kingdom of Judah (approximately 900 BCE).

And then there are the books of the prophets, those spokesmen for God whose words fired the Jewish conscience. Their names are immortal: Isaiah, Jeremiah, Ezekiel, Amos, Hosea, among others.

Someone once said: "There is no evidence of a biblical prophet ever being invited back a second time for dinner." Why? Because the prophets were tough. They had no patience for injustice, apathy, or hypocrisy. No one escaped their criticisms. Here's what they taught:

> God commands the Jews to behave decently toward one another. In fact, God cares more about basic ethics and decency than about ritual behavior.
> God chose the Jews *not* for special privileges, but for special duties to humanity.
> As bad as the Jews sometimes were, there was always the possibility that they would improve their behavior.
> As bad as things might be now, it will not always be that way. Someday, there will be universal justice and peace. Human history is moving forward toward an ultimate conclusion that some call the Messianic Age: a time of universal peace and prosperity for the Jewish people and for all the people of the world.

Your Mission—To Teach Torah to the Congregation

On the day when you become bar or bat mitzvah, you will be reading, or chanting, Torah—in Hebrew. You will be reading, or chanting, the haftarah—in Hebrew. That is the major skill that publicly marks the becoming of bar or bat mitzvah. But, perhaps even more important than that, you need to be able to teach something about the Torah portion, and perhaps the haftarah as well.

And that is where this book comes in. It will be a very valuable resource for you, and your family, in the b'nai mitzvah process.

Here is what you will find in it:

> A brief **summary** of every Torah portion. This is a basic overview of the portion; and, while it might not refer to everything in the Torah portion, it will explain its most important aspects.
> A list of the **major ideas** in the Torah portion. The purpose: to make the Torah portion real, in ways that we can relate to. Every Torah portion contains unique ideas, and when you put all

of those ideas together, you actually come up with a list of Judaism's most important ideas.

> Two *divrei Torah* ("words of Torah," or "sermonettes") for each portion. These *divrei Torah* explain significant aspects of the Torah portion in accessible, reader-friendly language. Each *devar Torah* contains references to **traditional** Jewish sources (those that were written before the modern era), as well as **modern** sources and quotes. We have searched, far and wide, to find sources that are unusual, interesting, and not just the "same old stuff" that many people already know about the Torah portion. Why did we include these minisermons in the volume? Not because we want you to simply copy those sermons and pass them off as your own (that would be cheating), though you are free to quote from them. We included them so that you can see what is possible—how you can try to make meaning for yourself out of the words of Torah.

> **Connections:** This is perhaps the most valuable part. It's a list of questions that you can ask yourself, or that others might help you think about—any of which can lead to the creation of your *devar Torah*.

Note: you don't have to like everything that's in a particular Torah portion. Some aren't that loveable. Some are hard to understand; some are about religious practices that people today might find confusing, and even offensive; some contain ideas that we might find totally outmoded.

But this doesn't have to get in the way. After all, most kids spend a lot of time thinking about stories that contain ideas that modern people would find totally bizarre. Any good medieval fantasy story falls into that category.

And we also believe that, if you spend just a little bit of time with those texts, you can begin to understand what the author was trying to say.

This volume goes one step further. Sometimes, the haftarah comes off as a second thought, and no one really thinks about it. We have tried to solve that problem by including a **summary** of each haftarah, and then a mini-sermon on the haftarah. This will help you learn how these sacred words are relevant to today's world, and even to your own life.

All Bible quotations come from the NJPS translation, which is found in the many different editions of the JPS TANAKH; in the Conservative movement's *Etz Hayim: Torah and Commentary;* in the Reform movement's *Torah: A Modern Commentary;* and in other Bible commentaries and study guides.

How Do I Write a *Devar Torah?*

It really is easier than it looks.

There are many ways of thinking about the *devar Torah.* It is, of course, a short sermon on the meaning of the Torah (and, perhaps, the haftarah) portion. It might even be helpful to think of the *devar Torah* as a "book report" on the portion itself.

The most important thing you can know about this sacred task is: *Learn* the words. *Love* the words. Teach people what it could mean to *live* the words.

Here's a basic outline for a *devar Torah:*

"My Torah portion is (name of portion) _____ ,
   from the book of _____ , chapter

   _____ .

"In my Torah portion, we learn that_____
   (Summary of portion)
"For me, the most important lesson of this Torah portion is (what is the best thing in the portion? Take the portion as a whole; your *devar Torah* does not have to be only, or specifically, on the verses that you are reading).
"As I learned my Torah portion, I found myself wondering:
   ‣ *Raise a question that the Torah portion itself raises.*
   ‣ *"Pick a fight"* with the portion. Argue with it.
   ‣ *Answer a question* that is listed in the "Connections" section of each Torah portion.
   ‣ *Suggest a question to your rabbi* that you would want the rabbi to answer in his or her own *devar Torah* or sermon.

"I have lived the values of the Torah by _____
(here, you can talk about how the Torah portion relates to your
own life. If you have done a mitzvah project, you can talk about
that here).

How To Keep It from Being Boring
(and You from Being Bored)

Some people just don't like giving traditional speeches. From our per-
spective, that's really okay. Perhaps you can teach Torah in a different
way—one that makes sense to you.

> Write an "open letter" to one of the characters in your Torah por-
  tion. "Dear Abraham: I hope that your trip to Canaan was not too
  hard . . ." "Dear Moses: Were you afraid when you got the Ten
  Commandments on Mount Sinai? I sure would have been . . ."
> Write a news story about what happens. Imagine yourself to
  be a television or news reporter. "Residents of neighboring cities were horrified yesterday as the wicked cities of Sodom and
  Gomorrah were burned to the ground. Some say that God was
  responsible . . ."
> Write an imaginary interview with a character in your Torah portion.
> Tell the story from the point of view of another character, or a mi-
  nor character, in the story. For instance, tell the story of the Garden of Eden from the point of view of the serpent. Or the story
  of the Binding of Isaac from the point of view of the ram, which
  was substituted for Isaac as a sacrifice. Or perhaps the story of
  the sale of Joseph from the point of view of his coat, which was
  stripped off him and dipped in a goat's blood.
> Write a poem about your Torah portion.
> Write a song about your Torah portion.
> Write a play about your Torah portion, and have some friends act
  it out with you.
> Create a piece of artwork about your Torah portion.

The bottom line is: Make this a joyful experience. Yes—it could
even be fun.

The Very Last Thing You Need to Know at This Point

The Torah scroll is written without vowels. Why? Don't *sofrim* (Torah scribes) know the vowels?

Of course they do.

So, why do they leave the vowels out?

One reason is that the Torah came into existence at a time when sages were still arguing about the proper vowels, and the proper pronunciation.

But here is another reason: The Torah text, as we have it today, and as it sits in the scroll, is actually *an unfinished work*. Think of it: the words are just sitting there. Because they have no vowels, it is as if they have no voice.

When we read the Torah publicly, we give voice to the ancient words. And when we find meaning in those ancient words, and we talk about those meanings, those words jump to life. They enter our lives. They make our world deeper and better.

Mazal tov to you, and your family. This is your journey toward Jewish maturity. Love it.

THE TORAH

❖ Balak: Numbers 22:2–25:9

After years of wandering in the wilderness, the Israelites are finally on their way toward the Promised Land. There have been many obstacles, including nations and tribes who have tried to get in their way.

But the Israelites have been victorious over them. That is why Balak, king of Moab, is frightened of the Israelites. Balak believes that the best way to fight them is not with swords, but with words. He hires a seer, Balaam, to curse Israel. This doesn't work out as well as Balak would have liked.

Summary

- The Israelites' victory over the Amorites has freaked out Balak, king of Moab. He sees that there are a great many Israelites, so he hires a seer, Balaam, to curse the Israelites, thinking that this will be effective in defeating them. God, however, has other plans for Balaam, and tells him not to curse the Israelites. Balaam refuses to go with Balak's emissaries but they are insistent and ultimately he agrees to go with them. (22:2–20)
- As Balaam begins his journey to curse the Israelites, he gets on his she-ass (donkey), who has other ideas about this trip. The donkey has a vision of an angel blocking their way. Balaam beats the animal into submission, and their trip continues. (Then the donkey starts talking!) (22:21–35)
- Balaam tries to curse the Israelites, but instead God forces him to utter blessings in the form of oracles (prophetic statements). In his first oracle, Balaam describes the Israelites as a people that dwells apart. (23:7–10)
- In his second oracle, Balaam says that God cannot be manipulated by magic or sorcery. (23:18–24)
- In his third oracle, Balaam goes one step further: not only will Israel not be cursed, but those who curse that nation will be cursed, and those who bless it will be blessed.
- In his fourth oracle, Balaam expands his view to include Moab and other nations, decreeing their ultimate fate. (24:3–25)

The Big Ideas

> **Words have power.** In ancient Judaism, blessings and curses were
> not just words. Ancient Jews believed that blessings and curses
> could actually shape the future. That is why Balak hired Balaam;
> his words could have been as powerful, or even more power-
> ful, than any military actions. This is true sometimes even today;
> what people say can both heal and hurt.

> **To be a Jew means to have vision.** In this sense, Balaam's don-
> key, who sees the angel even when he cannot, represents the Jew.
> Throughout their history, Jews have seen and understood things that
> other peoples have not. This has been a source of blessing to the
> Jewish people, and often a reason why some have not liked them.

> **To be Jewish sometimes means to be separate from other peo-
> ples.** Going back to ancient times, the Jewish people have often
> had to go it alone. Often, this was because other peoples perse-
> cuted them; at other times, some Jews have sensed that the best
> way to maintain their faith and culture was to separate themselves
> from others. Balaam's vision has, more often than not, been true.

> **God is not subject to magic.** The original meaning of "magic"
> was not the performance of a trick. It was to try to use certain
> rituals and techniques to manipulate the gods to get them to do
> what you want them to do. While other ancient peoples prac-
> ticed this kind of god-manipulation (in fact, this is precisely
> what Balak hired Balaam to do), one of the unique things about
> Judaism is that it never relied on these kinds of techniques.

> **The fate of the world is wrapped up in the fate of the Jews.** Ba-
> laam makes it clear that those who curse the Jews will be cursed
> and those who bless the Jews will be blessed. This echoes God's
> promise to Abram (Abraham) (Gen. 12:3). But he does not stop at
> the Jewish people. He expands his vision to include the nations
> that surround Israel. This reminds us that no nation is ever truly
> alone, because its actions always have impact on other countries.

Divrei Torah
LESSONS FROM A TALKING DONKEY

Here is one of the greatest and most wondrous aspects of children's literature: animals talk. Here's a short list: Charlotte, the spider in *Charlotte's Web;* Winnie the Pooh; Bugs Bunny; Donald Duck; Porky Pig; Teenage Mutant Ninja Turtles; Donkey in *Shrek;* and the Cowardly Lion in *The Wizard of Oz.* The list goes on and on. And it's not only in children's literature. Animals talk in mythical stories and folklore as well. And twice in the Torah: the serpent in the story of the Garden of Eden (Genesis 3), and the donkey in this Torah portion's story of Balaam.

And while this might seem a little childish, be careful; there is a great and powerful truth in this story.

Balaam, the Moabite soothsayer, is on his way to curse the Israelites. His mode of transportation is a donkey. God is not terribly interested in Balaam making his journey, and so God sends an angel to block Balaam's way. Here's the problem: Balaam cannot see the angel; only the donkey can. The animal walks off the path to avoid the angel, and Balaam hits her. Then, the angel appears in a narrow lane between two vineyard walls, and as the donkey presses against the wall she smashes Balaam's foot. Balaam hits the animal again. The third time, the angel chooses such a narrow place on the path that the animal has to lie down; and once again Balaam hits her. "Then the Lord opened the ass's mouth, and she said to Balaam, 'What have I done to you that you have beaten me these three times?' Balaam said to the ass, 'You have made a mockery of me! If I had a sword with me, I'd kill you'" (22:28–29).

A talking donkey: was this a miracle? No, said the ancient Rabbis—it was built into the very scheme of creation. "Ten things were created at twilight of the first eve of Shabbat—among them the mouth of Balaam's ass." Fine. But why do we even need the donkey in the story?

It's because the donkey sees the angel and has an understanding of God and the divine will. According to David Hazony: "The she-ass is Israel, possessing a divine truth, silently struggling under the lashes of power, driven by revelation to turn away from the path dictated by the violent overlords, eventually revealed and vindicated. Balaam, in turn, represents the nations of the world—perhaps the Egyptians who kept Israel enslaved through force. When the donkey finally speaks, asking what it has done to deserve being beaten, Balaam answers, 'Because you have mocked me.' Israel will always 'mock' the nations, just by refusing to follow the dictates of power."

There you have it—one of the most fascinating interpretations of any biblical story that you will ever read. The story teaches us that Jews understand that power is not the only way. And that is the truth they will continue to teach.

BEAUTIFUL TENTS

What are the first words Jews traditionally say when they enter a synagogue? "How fair are your tents, O Jacob, your dwellings, O Israel!" (24:5). They are part of the *Mah Tovu* prayer. It's an interesting choice when you consider that these opening words come to us from a Moabite soothsayer, Balaam, who had intended them to be words of cursing, and which God transformed into blessing. (Trivia point: this is the only Hebrew prayer by a non-Jew in the Jewish prayer book.)

But there is another reason why we say (or, as the case may be, sing) those words as we enter the synagogue. This author's own interpretation: Balaam praised the tents of the Jewish people, which were their homes. And Balaam also praised their dwellings, which are the synagogues that would someday exist.

Now, some people believe that you only need one, but not the other. Someday, you will probably meet Jews who say: "Why do I need the synagogue? I can pray in my home." They might say that, and it would be great if they did, in fact, pray in their homes, but they probably don't. And if there are no synagogues, what happens to the Jewish community?

Here's a way of thinking about it: Let's say that you're trying to get into shape, or training for a sport or an athletic competition. Sure, you can work out on your own, but you are more likely to have success if you do it with others, in a gym or outdoors. That's how Jewish communities work as well.

Rabbi David Teutsch writes: "A civilization cannot be handed down in privacy. It cannot be handed down just by reading books. To thrive, culture must be lived. . . . The setting for many important facets of Jewish civilization—eating, child-rearing, and Shabbat observance, for example—is the family. But the family cannot learn and sustain even these aspects of Jewish living by itself, and much of Judaism cannot be experienced just within the family. The only plausible setting for much of Jewish living is the community."

But, by the same token, Judaism cannot just be done in synagogue. It requires something to happen inside our homes as well. In fact, the best Jewish stuff happens around the table: Shabbat dinners, festival dinners, and Passover seders. That's what you remember every time you see a mezuzah on the doorpost of a Jewish house; the mezuzah is on a slant, pointing inside, to remind us that Judaism happens right there—inside the home.

So we need home and synagogue, family and community. A midrash teaches: "All the nations came to Balaam and asked, 'Can we take on this nation of Israel in battle?' He replied: 'Go out and make the rounds of their synagogues and houses of study. If you come upon children within them, chirping away in their childish voices, you will be unable to take on this nation in battle.'" Family *and* community are what make us strong.

Connections

> How have you come to understand that words have power? What words have been most powerful in your life?
> In what ways do Jews and the Jewish people remain separate from other peoples? Why has this happened? What are some of the benefits and disadvantages to this?
> In what ways have Jews and the Jewish people been part of the larger world? What's good about this? And maybe not so good?
> In what ways are the Jews like the talking animal in the story? What have Jews been able to see that other nations have not?
> Which do you think is more important and essential for the continuation of Judaism—the synagogue or the home? Why?

THE HAFTARAH

❖ Balak: Micah 5:6–6:8

Sometimes memories become distorted. Take the story of Balak, the Moabite king, and Balaam, the soothsayer, which is found in this week's Torah portion. You might think that the historical memory would record that Balaam tried to curse Israel but God transformed his curses into blessings. And, in fact, that is precisely what Jews remember about that incident, because Balaam's words, "How fair are your tents . . ." are the first words that Jews say (or sing) when they enter the synagogue.

But in the time of Micah, a prophet of the eighth century BCE, the "good" memory of that incident had not yet surfaced. No, for Micah, the incident was wholly negative. The prophet recalls "what Balak king of Moab plotted against you" (6:5).

According to Micah, God will not only destroy Israel's enemies, but will also wreak havoc on Israel's own idolatrous practices. This is the essence of the prophet's message: God is not terribly interested in Israel's pious sacrifices. Above everything else, God wants ethical behavior—as expressed in Micah's famous verse: "He has told you, O man, what is good, and what the Lord requires of you: only to do justice, and to love goodness, and to walk modestly with your God" (6:8).

Read That Again, Please

We find these words, written across the doors and *bimah*s of countless synagogues all over the world. "He has told you, O man, what is good, and what the Lord requires of you: only to do justice, and to love goodness, and to walk modestly with your God" (6:8).

It has practically become a cliché, which would be a good reason for us to ask ourselves: What does it really mean, especially the part about walking modestly?

This verse is so important that it was even imagined to be one of the great summaries of all Judaism. "Micah reduced the mitzvot to those three principles . . . [including] 'walking modestly with your God,' that is, walking in funeral and bridal processions." Rabbi Simlai, the talmudic sage and author of this statement, fleshed out the meaning of "walking modestly" in an interesting and unusual way: the mitzvah of attending funerals and weddings—of being with people at sad times and at joyous moments. Taking the time to simply be with people in their hour of need; not necessarily saying anything, but just being there for them, is a true act of humility.

The biblical scholar Professor David Sperling offers another interpretation: "Be aware that, in the presence of God, we are only human." Act with self-restraint. Don't show off. To be modest is to know our limitations.

There is an alternative way to translate and understand the first phrase of Micah's statement: *Higid lekha adam mah tov, u-mah Adonai elohekha doreish mimkha.* This is how it is rendered over the *bimah* at the Liberal Jewish Synagogue in London: "Man might have told you what is good, but what does God require of you?"

That unique translation imagines a dialogue between what people think is important, and what God knows is important. "Man" (human beings) might tell you that sacrifices are important, but God requires ethical behavior.

Or, perhaps it means something even more radical. Don't pay attention to what society says. Know that there are greater ideals out there, a deeper reality. In the words of psychiatrist and author Silvano Arieti: "People continue to see the Jew as an iconoclast, as the one who has destroyed their most cherished beliefs. The Jew not only challenges their ideas, but he places in doubt what for them has counted most."

To be Jewish is to strive for the ethical no matter what the circumstances. To be Jewish is to listen to God, even more than you listen to people. Now, that is a challenge!

❖ Notes

❖ Notes